At David C Cook, we equip the local church around the corner and around the globe to make disciples. Come see how we are working together—go to **www.davidccook.org**. Thank you!

transforming lives together

Sean McDowell
and
J. Warner Wallace

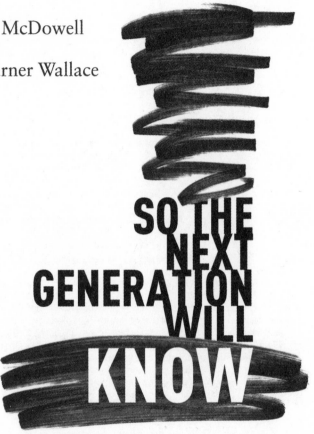

SO THE
NEXT
GENERATION
WILL
KNOW

Preparing Young Christians
for a Challenging World

PARTICIPANT'S GUIDE

DAVID C COOK
transforming lives together

SO THE NEXT GENERATION WILL KNOW PARTICIPANT'S GUIDE
Published by David C Cook
4050 Lee Vance Drive
Colorado Springs, CO 80918 U.S.A.

Integrity Music Limited, a Division of David C Cook
Brighton, East Sussex BN1 2RE, England

The graphic circle C logo is a registered trademark of David C Cook.

The website addresses recommended throughout this book are offered as a resource to you. These websites are not intended in any way to be or imply an endorsement on the part of David C Cook, nor do we vouch for their content.

Details in some stories have been changed to protect
the identities of the persons involved.

Unless otherwise noted, all Scripture quotations are taken from the ESV® Bible (The Holy Bible, English Standard Version®), copyright © 2001 by Crossway, a publishing ministry of Good News Publishers. Used by permission. All rights reserved. Scripture quotations marked NASB are taken from the New American Standard Bible®, copyright © 1960, 1995 by The Lockman Foundation. Used by permission. (www.Lockman.org). The authors have added italics to Scripture quotations for emphasis.

ISBN 978-1-4347-1229-5
eISBN 978-0-8307-7718-1

© 2019 James Warner Wallace and Sean McDowell
Published in association with the literary agency of Mark
Sweeney & Associates, Naples, FL 34113.

The Team: Timothy Fox, Stephanie Bennett, Amy Konyndyk,
Jack Campbell, Susan Murdock
Cover Design: Nick Lee

Printed in the United States of America
First Edition 2019

2 3 4 5 6 7 8 9 10 11

102419

THE AUTHORS

Sean McDowell, PhD, is an associate professor of Christian apologetics at Talbot School of Theology, Biola University, as well as a part-time high school teacher at Capistrano Valley Christian Schools. He is a bestselling author (or coauthor) of more than eighteen books, including *A New Kind of Apologist*.

Sean is a popular speaker at camps, conferences, universities, and churches worldwide. He is also the National Spokesman for Summit Ministries, a worldview training ministry for students sixteen to twenty-five. Sean lives in Southern California with his wife and three kids. You can learn more about Sean McDowell's ministry at SeanMcDowell.org.

J. Warner Wallace is a *Dateline*-featured cold-case detective, Senior Fellow at the Colson Center for Christian Worldview, adjunct professor of Christian apologetics at Talbot School of Theology, Biola University, and faculty member at Summit Worldview Conference. He is the author of *Cold-Case Christianity*, *God's Crime Scene*, and *Forensic Faith*, and is the creator (along with his wife, Susie) of the Case Makers Academy for Kids (CaseMakersAcademy.com).

J. Warner served as a children's minister, youth pastor, and lead pastor before becoming a popular national speaker. He and Susie live in Southern California and have four grown children. You can learn more about J. Warner's ministry at ColdCaseChristianity.com.

CONTENTS

Session 1

LOVE *RESPONDS*
EXAMINING THE CHALLENGE BEFORE US

Challenges require a response, and the church is facing a *true challenge*: young people in America and Europe are leaving the Christian church at an unprecedented rate.

I (J. Warner) first noticed the problem when I was a youth pastor. I took over leadership from my energetic, young predecessor, who had grown the group into a robust, engaged collection of junior high and high school students. Many had been raised together in the church, and they invited their friends to join the group. As a result, our students had deep relationships that bound them together.

In my first year as their pastor, I leaned heavily on my training as an artist (I have a BA in design and an MA in architecture). Our meetings were interactive, artistic, and experiential, incorporating music, imagery, and other sensory elements. The students seemed to enjoy the approach, and over time the group grew even larger.

But our results were *terrible*.

Not long after graduating the first seniors, we found that most of them walked away from Christianity in the initial weeks of their freshman year at college. Many of our current students were still in touch with these new nonbelievers, and when I heard that they now rejected the existence of God, I was crushed, and I accepted the blame.

In the year since becoming their pastor, I had come to *love* these students. I felt a paternal responsibility to them. Like the apostle John, I wanted "no greater joy than this, to hear of my children walking in the truth" (3 John 1:4 NASB). When I heard that most of my graduating seniors had strayed from the family, I reconciled myself to the fact that I hadn't adequately prepared them for life after youth group. I thought, *I must be the worst youth pastor ever*. Then I started to study the issue more deeply and found that I wasn't alone.

If you're a youth pastor, Christian educator, or parent, I bet you've got a story of your own about a young ex-believer you love who was raised in the church. We've all got a student, son, daughter, grandson, granddaughter, niece, or nephew who has walked away from the truth. This isn't just an anecdotal problem. It's a national crisis. And it's also *personal*. Everywhere we travel, we hear heartbreaking stories from caring adults who know young people who have abandoned their faith. It can be especially hard when these are *our own kids*.

Let's explore what we can do to keep our kids in the faith.

THINK ABOUT THE NEXT GENERATION

1. Do you have a friend or loved one who abandoned their faith? If so, what do you believe were the main contributing factor(s)?

2. Why do you think that so many teens and young adults disengage from the church?

3. What do you think the church is doing—or *isn't* doing—that contributes to this?

4. Reflect on your teenage years.
    What was your experience with Christianity?

    Was your view of those of older generations mainly positive or negative, and why?

    If you were a Christian in your teenage years, did you have a spiritual mentor in your life, or did you wish that you did? If so, what role did he or she play in your faith journey?

WATCH THE VIDEO AND TAKE NOTES
1. We _____ for what we love.

2. What are the two mistakes people make in response to Gen Z's disconnect with Christianity?

3. The main barriers to belief fall into what two categories?

4. What is the number one statistical factor for why a child would embrace the faith of his or her family?

5. What is the connection between truth and relationship?

6. What is the current "age of skepticism," and how are children introduced to skepticism?

RESPOND IN YOUR OWN WORDS

1. Young people have always drifted from the church. But we've learned that Gen Z is leaving in greater numbers than any generation before. Why do you think this is the case?

2. We've also learned that Gen Z is disconnecting from the church *at an earlier age* than previous generations.

Does this fact surprise you?

What do you believe are the contributing factors for this?

3. What are the biggest questions or doubts that you have about your Christian faith? Are they different from the kinds of questions you had as a young person?

What are you doing to address them?

4. What do you think are the most pressing faith questions that our kids have?

What do you think are the sources for their questions and doubts?

Where are they going for answers? Where did you go with your questions?

THE REASONS ARE REVEALING

Researchers have been asking young ex-Christians *why* they have left the church, and their answers are enlightening. Here are some popular student responses from different studies:

"Too many questions that can't be answered."[1]
"I learned about evolution when I went away to college."
"There is a lack of any sort of scientific or specific evidence of a creator."
"I just realized somewhere along the line that I didn't really believe it."

"Because I grew up and realized it was a story like Santa or the Easter Bunny."

"I have a hard time believing that a good God would allow so much evil or suffering in the world."

"There are too many injustices in the history of Christianity."

"I had a bad experience at church with a Christian."[2]

Most of these responses involve some form of *unanswered, intellectual skepticism*. Young believers struggle to answer tough questions from a Christian perspective, and young people in general are seeking a reasonable worldview that makes sense of reality.

1. How many of those responses do *you* feel adequately equipped to answer?

2. Which response do you find most challenging to answer?

How does it affect you when you don't have an answer?

Do you think it affects young people differently? Why or why not? And if so, how?

3. This lesson stressed the importance of connecting truth and relationships. Why do you think this connection is important?

What are some practical ways we can better improve this connection?

CONNECTING TRUTH AND RELATIONSHIPS

When we encourage parents to become the best Christian apologists their kids will ever know, we do so because we understand the connection between truth and relationships. Given this reality, here are a few suggestions based on the data we've already described:

- **Make a Commitment:** Each of us, in our own small way, can contribute to the important work of raising the next generation of Christians if we will simply *commit ourselves* to the task.

- **Start Early:** According to the statistics, young Christians decide to abandon the church long before they ever tell anyone and usually before they leave the homes of their parents. It's tempting to think your church's high school youth ministry will eventually address intellectual skepticism, but the data tells a different story. We must start much earlier.
- **Take on the Tough Issues:** Imagine getting some of these questions from the young Christians in your life:

  "What scientific proof do you have that God exists?"
  "If evolution is true, why should I believe in God?"
  "How is believing in God any different from believing in Santa Claus or the Easter Bunny?"
  "Why does science seem to contradict the claims of Christianity?"
  "Why would an all-powerful, all-loving God allow so much evil in the world?"
  "How can I be sure Jesus really rose from the grave?"
  "Why should I care about any of this to begin with?"

The data tells us that these are *precisely* the kinds of questions we need to be prepared to answer if we want to help young people find the truth and follow the Savior.

- **Be Patient:** Be patient with yourself if you don't seem to have all the right answers or if the young people you're leading don't seem to be progressing as quickly as you might like.

- **Stay Balanced:** Our instruction—especially toward those who are younger—is a vehicle for truth, fueled by loving relationships. Our challenge is to avoid tilting our approach too far in either direction.

It shouldn't surprise us that the secret to Christian education is based on this connection between truth and relationships. Remember that our model for teaching apologetics and Christian worldview is anchored and rooted in a uniquely Christian approach that unites truth to relationship, law to grace, justice to mercy.

From your own experience, do you think your children or students struggle more with the truth or relational aspect of Christianity?

Do you think relational experiences shape intellectual doubts? If so, how?

PAUSE FOR PERSONAL ASSESSMENT

1. After this lesson, do you feel discouraged or hopeful about Gen Z?

2. Just the fact that you are participating in this study shows that you care about the next generation. What are some concrete ways that we can sacrifice for the ones we love to help them remain connected to Christ?

3. Do you think your personal strength is in relaying truth or building relationships? What can you do to improve the balance between the two?

4. What was your biggest takeaway from this lesson?

MAKE A PLAN

We make time for what is important to us. Look at your schedule and see how you can carve out time to study the tough objections that face Gen Z, as well as to establish a deeper relationship with your children or students. Remember that we sacrifice for what we love. You'll need to make changes in your schedule if you want to make a difference for this generation. Whether it's an hour a day or an hour a week, be intentional about how you use your time.

1. As a result of this lesson, what are two action steps you can take?

2. What resources are available to help you respond to tough objections to Christianity?

3. Who can you lean on for support and assistance?

Based on your role with Gen Z, the following are some further suggestions on how to better engage their concerns:

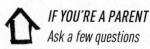

IF YOU'RE A PARENT
Ask a few questions

We sometimes take the spiritual growth of our kids for granted. Although they may continue to attend church with us, they may be far less committed to (or interested in) Christianity and also be reluctant to share their concerns and doubts.

Begin asking important questions, even at an early age:

- "What do you think is the most difficult thing to believe about Christianity?"
- "Of all the things the pastor said today, what seemed the most difficult to believe?"
- "What is your biggest question or doubt about Christianity?"
- "What do your skeptical friends say about Christianity?"

Don't rush to respond. Instead, be a good listener and use the data you collect to structure and inspire your own studies. And be sure to communicate in both your words and your body language that you are okay with their questions and doubts.

IF YOU'RE A YOUTH PASTOR OR MINISTER
Present a few questions

Youth group can be an intimidating place for students to ask questions or reveal what they really think about Christianity, especially if we haven't cultivated a ministry that embraces doubt.

Try implementing a "You Ask It Bag" in which students can place their questions, anonymously, about anything they want answered. The bag accomplishes two goals. First, it allows students to ask questions safely. Second, it provides an incentive for our youth workers and volunteers to prepare themselves with good answers.

IF YOU'RE A CHRISTIAN EDUCATOR
Poll your students

Invite your students to raise questions during one of your classes, or ask them to submit their questions anonymously. Consider asking for responses to such topics as: "If you could ask God one question, what would it be?" or "If you could ask God to explain one confusing thing, what would it be?"

As you're publicly recognizing and charting the questions, acknowledge the validity of investigating in the first place. Let your classroom be a place where these kinds of questions and discussions are welcome.

GATHER YOUR THOUGHTS

Every generation has faced a disconnect with Christianity during their teenage years. But as we've learned, Gen Z is disconnecting at an earlier age and in greater numbers. These facts can cause us to be overly alarmist or we can chalk it up to "kids being kids." Let's avoid both mistakes. Because you love this generation, make it a point to be intentional about reconnecting them with their faith. Try to engage them on both an emotional level *and* an intellectual level. We must balance relationship and truth. And remember that God is on your side. As much as you love Gen Z, God loves them even more. Let that be your comfort and your strength.

> But in your hearts honor Christ the Lord as holy, always being prepared to make a defense to anyone who asks you for a reason for the hope that is in you; yet do it with gentleness and respect. (1 Peter 3:15)

INCREASE YOUR UNDERSTANDING

This session is based on the *So the Next Generation Will Know* book, chapter 1, "Love *Responds*." For more ideas on how to build relationships and instill truth in the next generation, read the section A Biblical Way Forward, jotting down notes on J. Warner's and Sean's personal experiences.

Some notes from J. Warner's experiences:

Some notes from Sean's experiences:

LOVE *UNDERSTANDS*
RECOGNIZING THE UNIQUENESS OF THIS GENERATION

I (Sean) grew up with parents on Cru staff (formerly Campus Crusade for Christ). Because my parents are well known and have built relationships with people in Cru over a number of decades, other staff members regularly ask me how my parents are doing. And I am more than happy to oblige them.

One time as a high school student, when I was at Cru Staff Training in Fort Collins, Colorado, a staff member named Mike asked how I was doing personally. Assuming he really wanted to know about my parents, I proceeded to tell him what they were up to. But he cut me off mid-sentence and said, "I'm not asking about your parents. I am interested in *you*. How are *you* doing? Tell me about *your story*." It caught me off guard. And I soon realized he was totally sincere. He was interested in knowing about my interests, dreams, and goals and not simply because of who my parents were. He was interested in understanding *me*.

Looking back over my years as a Cru staff kid, Mike had a big influence on my life. He invited me to weekend retreats and various events, and he always made a point to connect with me personally.

One of the big reasons he was able to speak into my life was because he began by desiring to understand me as a person. Rather than importing assumptions from my family, my age, or where I was from, he made it clear that he wanted to understand me as a person.

When we truly love someone, we aim to understand that person. The challenge is that it takes time and effort. This is not only true for friends, neighbors, and coworkers, but it is especially true for the next generation of young people. If we truly want to love them, we must make the commitment to understand them first.

THINK ABOUT THE NEXT GENERATION

1. Write down the first words that come to mind when you think of Gen Z.

2. What are some words to describe your generation?

What are the major *events* that impacted your generation?

3. What are some traits that are common to teenagers across all generations?

What are the differences between Gen Z and previous generations?

WATCH THE VIDEO AND TAKE NOTES

1. It's more important to _____ than to be _____.

2. Impacts of Gen Z being digital natives:

3. Principles for engaging Gen Z:

RESPOND IN YOUR OWN WORDS

In many ways, all teenagers across all generations are the same. But every generation has its own unique events and characteristics that shape it. Gen Z is no different. There are many things that are unique to this generation, due to time and technology. So we need to take the time to understand the issues and concerns that make this generation who they are.

1. Look back at your list of words to describe Gen Z. Are they mostly positive or negative? If they are mostly negative, why do you think that is the case? What might that reveal about *you*?

2. What are the unique characteristics of Gen Z?

3. Gen Z are "digital natives." They're using smartphones before they can read. What are the positive and negative impacts of this trend?

4. We learned that 79 percent—nearly 4 out of 5—Gen Zers feel distressed when they are away from their smartphones.

Does this statistic surprise you? Why or why not?

Have you personally experienced this response from a Gen Zer?

Let's try to understand how Gen Z sees the world so that we can love them uniquely for who they are. Researchers studying Gen Z typically list several important observations and findings about this segment of our Christian family. Here are a few:

They're Researchers

Gen Z is continually connected to the internet. They know precisely where to go to research any variety of topics, and they can do so very quickly. As a result, they understand how to educate themselves and find their own answers.

They're Visual Multitaskers

The most popular social media apps Gen Zers use on their smart-phones are entirely visual, video (or image) based platforms. They're also able to divide their attention repeatedly by multitasking between visual platforms.

They're Impatient

Gen Zers have been raised in an age in which speed and convenience rule the day. They expect instantaneous delivery on nearly everything from information to music to goods.

They're Fluid

Technology has contributed to a blurring of the lines between work and home, truth and fiction, fact and feeling, and our public and private lives. Few believe there is such a thing as a "normal" family. Formerly fixed categories of gender have increasingly broken down in the minds of Gen Z.

They're Social Justice Oriented

Unlike prior generations that embraced anti-establishment causes (i.e., Baby Boomers) or environmental causes (i.e., Millennials), Gen

Zers are motivated by causes surrounding *human equality*. These include issues related to poverty, human trafficking, refugees, and more.

They're Individualistic

Young people today have grown up in a culture that places the individual as the highest authority. Gen Zers resist judging the moral choices of others, and individual feelings often trump facts.

They're Transparent

Authenticity is important to Gen Z. They seek real relationships, and they respect transparency. They know people aren't perfect. They want to hear personal stories that reveal imperfections and weaknesses, because they know *they* have similar vulnerabilities.

They're Post-Christian

More young Americans describe themselves as religiously unaffiliated than ever before. The frequency of Bible reading, prayer, and church attendance is also declining. The Bible no longer holds the same authority in the minds of this generation.

For more detail on these characteristics and more not listed here, see *So the Next Generation Will Know*, pages 52–59.

5. Which of these characteristics have you noticed in the lives of your children or students?

Can you think of any other major characteristics that are not listed here or mentioned in the video?

6. Which one characteristic do you think is Gen Z's greatest strength?

Which single characteristic concerns you most?

PRINCIPLES FOR INTERACTING WITH GEN Z

Now let's examine three *timeless* principles we can apply as we interact with Gen Z:

Remember, every young person has a unique story.

Focus on what we have in common rather than what separates us.

Stay positive and don't dwell on negative aspects of the younger generation.

Reflect on the specific Gen Zers in your life using these three principles.

In what ways do they differ from the standard characteristics of their generation?

What do you have in common with them? Try to be as specific as possible.

What are their positive aspects?

If you found it difficult to answer those questions, don't be discouraged! Use that as motivation to get to know the Gen Zers in your life better. Occasionally reflect on these three questions and see if you are making progress in understanding the next generation.

PAUSE FOR PERSONAL ASSESSMENT

1. In the video, Sean said, "How you view a generation will affect how you relate to them." Do you personally find it difficult to stay positive about Gen Z? Why or why not?

2. Reflect on when you were a teenager:
   How were your relationships with people from older generations, especially with those who are your age now?

What similarities are there between you as a teenager and Gen Z?

How can you leverage this to better relate to your children or students?

3. Because of this session, has your attitude toward Gen Z changed? If so, how?

4. What was your biggest takeaway from this session?

MAKE A PLAN

Just as we resolved in the last session, we must intentionally carve time out of our busy schedules to understand the young people in our lives. Ask them about their day, their interests, their dislikes. You may learn something new, and you may realize that you have more in common with them than you think. But your interest must be genuine! Let them know that you aren't trying to "fix" them but that you are genuinely interested in them. As we've learned, transparency and authenticity is very important to Gen Z. If you are real to them with your experiences and struggles, they will be more open to share their lives with you. Love understands.

1. List one or two specific Gen Zers whom you will resolve to get to know better this week.

2. What concrete steps will you take to understand them better?

3. How can you leverage the characteristics of Gen Z listed earlier to better connect with young people?

4. In the video, Sean said, "Previous generations learned how to communicate online. This generation—as a whole—has to learn how to communicate offline." What are some concrete ways that you can help the Gen Zers in your life learn how to connect to others offline, or face to face?

IF YOU'RE A PARENT
Ask a few questions

Consider taking your kids out for coffee, ice cream, or a meal (possibly as you pick them up after school) and asking them these questions (or ones like them). Tell them you just want to listen so you can become a better mom or dad:

- If you had a free day to do anything, what would you do?
- What are your favorite memories of our family?
- How would you describe our family to an outsider?
- Are there some things other families do that you wish we did together?
- What are your favorite things to do with me?
- If you were me, what changes would you make to our family?
- Do you want to be a parent someday?
- Is there anything I do that frustrates you?
- What is one thing I could do to be a better dad (or mom) to you?

This will help show your willingness and desire to be a better parent. There is another reason this is important: Gen Zers highly value authenticity. They don't expect perfection, and they respond when we are real.

IF YOU'RE A YOUTH PASTOR OR MINISTER
Seek to understand your students

Invite your students to share their stories with you. You might provide these prompts on a board or project them on a screen:

- Whether or not you believe in God, describe your faith story.
- If you could ask God one question, what would it be? Why?
- What can you share with me from your story to help me best understand who you are today?

Get students sharing so you can know them better. You might be surprised how much some students are willing to talk about their lives when given the chance to write their reflections. Consider writing students a personal letter in response, letting them know that you are praying for them and available anytime (talk or text).

IF YOU'RE A CHRISTIAN EDUCATOR
Poll your students

Simply ask the questions below, or ones like them, and record their answers on the board. Let them know your goal is to understand them more clearly so you can better relate to them:

- What characteristics best describe your generation?
- Who are the most influential voices to your generation (i.e., YouTubers, artists, athletes, etc.)?
- What makes your generation different from previous generations?
- What are the most common misunderstandings older generations have about you?
- What are the collective experiences that help define your generation?
- What is hardest about being a young person today?
- What makes students in our school unique from those in other schools?

- If you could give leaders advice, what would it be?

When you finish this activity, ask if you can share these insights with other teachers, staff members, administrators, and parents. Assure them that you will not reveal individual answers, but that you simply want to share key trends.

GATHER YOUR THOUGHTS

If we want to impact Gen Z, we need to understand them. Think back to your teenage years, on what was most important to you. Many of the same things may be important to Gen Z as well. But also remember that this generation has its own strengths and weaknesses. And don't forget that every *individual* within Gen Z is unique. Get to know your children and students. Learn the general needs of Gen Z as well as their specific needs as individuals.

> By wisdom a house is built, and by understanding it is established. (Proverbs 24:3)

INCREASE YOUR UNDERSTANDING

To better understand how to interact with Gen Z, read the final pages of *So the Next Generation Will Know*, chapter 2, "Love *Understands*." Focus on the paragraphs dealing with interaction, and take notes for the following sections:

Remember, Every Young Person Has a Unique Story
How are young people distinct and unique in their use of social media?

Focus on What We Have in Common

What biblical truths unite us, regardless of our age, race, or status?

Stay Positive

How does our description of Gen Z act as a lens through which we understand and relate to this generation?

Session 3

LOVE *RELATES*
CONNECTING WITH THE HEARTS OF YOUNG PEOPLE

"Dad, I'm not sure if I believe in Christianity. I want to know what is true, but I have a lot of questions."

What would *you* say if your son or daughter spoke these words to you? How would you respond if these words came from a young Christian you deeply cared about? Well, as a nineteen-year-old college student, I (Sean) spoke these words to my father, not knowing how he would respond, especially since I was questioning the very *message* he has committed his life to proclaiming.

And yet I will never forget my father's confident response: "Son, I am glad to see you exploring your faith seriously, because you can't live on my convictions. You have to know for yourself what you think is true. If you genuinely seek truth, I am confident you will follow Jesus, because He is the truth. Only walk away from what you have learned growing up if you conclude it is false. And know that your mom and I will love you no matter what you believe."

Not long ago, I decided to ask my dad how he was *really* feeling when I told him about my doubt years earlier, assuming he must have been deeply concerned at the time. Was he worried I might abandon my faith? What was actually going through his mind?

His response caught me off guard. He told me that he wasn't worried about my faith journey because of the depth of our *relationship*. While he believes the evidence for Christianity is compelling, it was our relationship that gave him confidence I would stay in the faith. There were certainly no guarantees, of course, and my dad is endlessly optimistic by nature, but his response illustrates a point we want to drive home in this book: *truth is best learned and sustained in relationship*.

If we want the next generation to come to know the faith, we have to teach, model, and incarnate truth in our relationship with them. It is not truth *or* relationship—it is truth *and* relationship.

THINK ABOUT THE NEXT GENERATION

1. How often is your family able to gather for meals together?

Does your family engage in conversations, or is it more like "eat and run"?

What is the role of electronic devices at the dinner table?

2. What do you think are the most common things vying for Gen Zers' attention and devotion?

3. Did you have a spiritual mentor in your younger years? If so, how much of an impact did this person have on your life?

WATCH THE VIDEO AND TAKE NOTES

1. What are some relational counterfeits competing for Gen Z's attention?

2. List strategies for connecting with Gen Z:

RESPOND IN YOUR OWN WORDS

Each day multiple things vie for our attention, whether it is TV, YouTube, or social media. The same is true for Gen Z. It's different for them, however, because they are digital natives. They don't have the perspective of knowing what life without smartphones is like, and how to manage their technology use responsibly.

While the internet and prevalence of smartphones make it easier than ever to connect with others, why are Gen Zers still so lonely?

Besides technology, what are some other things that may contribute to Gen Z's loneliness?

A LONELY GENERATION

As we saw in session 2, loneliness is a defining feature of young people, including Christians, today. When healthy relationships are lacking, young people experience a vacuum they will seek to fill with a relational counterfeit. This lonely generation will search for something to fill their relational hole, and many of our culture's options can easily become addictive.

Let's consider some of the relational counterfeits vying for the hearts of Gen Z:

Consumerism

Commercials, social media promotions, and celebrities promise that if young people just buy a certain product, their lives will be filled. The incessant exposure to advertisements sends the message that young people are missing out and *need* a consumer item for fulfillment.

Busyness

With social media, YouTube, television, and more, it is possible to never get bored. But *why* is this generation so busy and distracted? It is much easier to live in a state of distraction than to confront the loneliness in the human heart.

Pornography

Pornography is epidemic with young people. It removes vulnerability, which is necessary for real love. It makes sex cheap, easy, and relationship-free. The smiling porn star promises to fulfill all of your fantasies and will never reject you.

Social Media

People need *embodied* relationships. We crave appropriate touch, eye contact, and human presence. Social media can help foster connections in remarkable ways, but it cannot replace our need for actual relationships.

Video Games

Young people look to video games in order to fill their hearts with meaning and significance. Many video games are designed to subtly promise respect, community, identity, and control—the very things many youth are searching for.

God designed us for relationships, and when they are lacking, *something* will fill the void. Broken relationships are at the heart of why this generation has so many addictions.

1. How many of these relational counterfeits have you turned to in your life?

How much more do you think they affect Gen Z? Do you believe they are more susceptible to these deceptions? Why or why not?

2. What do the five relational counterfeits we looked at have in common that is so intriguing to lonely, immature young adults?

3. Can you think of any other relational counterfeits that vie for Gen Zers' attention? And how do these compare and contrast with relational counterfeits vying for the hearts of adults?

FIVE STRATEGIES FOR CONNECTING WITH GENERATION Z

Here are some strategies we have found helpful in building relationships with young people:

Share Stories

Stories shape how we view the world, and they allow us to be known by a young person. Describe special memories about your upbringing, your work, and your hobbies. Be vulnerable, and share both your successes and your failures. You don't have to tell your entire life story to a young person, but let him or her know you can relate to them by sharing your relevant life experiences and struggles.

Enter Your Kids' World

It is impossible to truly know young people until you see things from their perspective. Watch their movie of choice. Listen to their music. Eat at a restaurant they enjoy. Play a video game with them. This not only shows that you value them but gives you a glimpse into their dreams and desires as well. Rather than merely inviting them into your world, go into theirs.

Be a Good Listener

For a distracted and impatient generation, listening can be one of our best ways to connect. Good listening expresses, "You are important to me. I want to understand you, so I can respond in a caring manner." Ask genuine questions. Give eye contact. Show empathy. And try to genuinely understand *before* you speak.

Mentor a Young Person

Mentoring can be as simple as bringing a young person along with you on the tasks you already do. It could involve taking one of your students with you to the store or finding a young person who also enjoys working out.

Have a Conversation

Young people today just want someone to talk to. Are you willing to have a conversation with a young person and help fill his or her deep need for relationship?

1. Think back to when you were young. If you had a mentor in your life, which of these relational strategies did he or she employ?

2. These ideas for connection aren't just practical; they're biblical. What stories in the Bible involve people sharing a meal together?

Why do you think the act of sharing a meal is so significant?

PAUSE FOR PERSONAL ASSESSMENT

1. Think back to Sean sharing his crisis of faith with his father at the beginning of the session. If your own children were to tell you that they doubted their faith, how do you think you would react?

Do you think your relationship with them is strong enough that you could trust them to honestly seek the truth on their own?

Do you think your children would feel comfortable enough to tell you they were having doubts? How can you ensure the lines of communication remain open?

Do you think this crisis of faith would put a strain on your relationship? Why or why not?

What are some unhelpful ways parents respond when their kids question their faith? What are some helpful responses?

2. Have you ever used the excuse of being "too old" or "too out of touch" to avoid building a relationship with a young person?

3. How have the distractions of life, especially technology, negatively impacted your own relationships?

4. What was your biggest takeaway from this lesson?

MAKE A PLAN

1. What concrete steps are you going to take to ensure relational counterfeits don't interfere with your and your family's relationships? For example, scheduling screen-free times, not allowing devices at the dinner table, etc.

2. If the next generation is going to have healthy relationships with others, they first need to know what a healthy relationship looks like. How can you better model healthy relationships to the young people in your life?

3. Commit yourself to improving a relationship with just one young person this week. Which one or two strategies will you employ to do so?

Based on your role with Gen Z, here are some further suggestions on how to better establish a relationship with a young person:

IF YOU'RE A PARENT
Imagine a few scenarios

Our kids will let us down. But what we often fail to do is prepare ahead of time for how we might respond to their failures so we can minister to them biblically, and in love, when the time comes. For instance, have you considered the following questions?

- What if I discover one of my kids is looking at porn?
- What if my son is caught cheating on a test at school?
- How would I respond if I discovered one of my kids was smoking weed?
- What would I do if one of my kids sexted another student?
- How would I respond if my son or daughter bullied another student or is bullied by one?
- What if my daughter gets pregnant?

The best way to respond with truth and grace is to plan beforehand how we will react to this news if it comes. The goal is to respond lovingly and firmly so as to preserve the relationship but also guide our kids to authentic healing. Take a few moments and reflect on how you might respond in these situations.

IF YOU'RE A YOUTH PASTOR OR MINISTER
Make sure you have the facts

Members of Gen Z research everything. They have access to unlimited information at their fingertips and can check any story or claim you make in your teaching. Thus, to build trust with this generation, it is more important than ever to get your facts right. If you get things wrong, you will lose credibility, and thus your voice, to genuinely influence this generation. Consider a few questions about yourself:

- Do you do your homework in preparation for speaking?
- When speaking on a subject, do you qualify the strength of your claims to the strength of the evidence?
- Do you offer alternative perspectives to your students and critique them fairly?
- Do you admit when you are not an expert on a topic and provide someone who is?
- Are you willing to admit when you are wrong?

 ### *IF YOU'RE A CHRISTIAN EDUCATOR*
Make yourself available

We know you are busy with lesson plans, grading, extracurricular activities, and the other myriads of responsibilities teachers inherit. But how available are you for your students? If you want to meaningfully speak truth into their lives, communicate your accessibility through your words and actions. Consider a few questions:

- Do you tell your students that you are available for help outside the classroom?
- Are you welcoming when students first enter the room?
- Do you know their names and use them?
- Do you leave your classroom during the day to connect with students around campus?
- Do you attend school functions, such as sporting events and plays, to convey that you value students' lives?
- Do you express genuine interest in the lives of your students outside the classroom?

GATHER YOUR THOUGHTS

As the saying goes, people don't care how much you know until they know how much you care. Gen Z is no different. They want people to be genuine and transparent with them. However, Gen Z may be the loneliest generation ever. Facebook friends and Instagram followers cannot replace a real, in-person relationship. Be intentional about establishing relationships with the young people in your life. Let them know that you honestly care about them and want what's best for them. Love relates.

Be quick to hear, slow to speak. (James 1:19)

INCREASE YOUR UNDERSTANDING

We've only discussed five of ten strategies for connecting with Gen Z. Read *So the Next Generation Will Know*, chapter 3, "Love *Relates*," focusing on Ten Strategies for Connecting with Generation Z on pages 72–77. Take notes on the five strategies *not* described in this participant's guide:

Practice _____:

Express _____:

Set Reasonable _____:

Pray:

Share a _____:

Of the ten strategies listed, which ones are you most successfully employing with the young people in your lives?

Which strategies would you like to improve on?

Session 4

LOVE *EQUIPS*
GIVING KIDS A WORLDVIEW THAT BRINGS SIGNIFICANCE

Surfing looks easy. How hard can it be to stand on a board and ride down a wave? I (Sean) remember thinking this shortly before I went surfing the first time as a junior high student. My friends tried to warn me and prepare me for the challenges of learning how to surf, but I recall thinking, *No worries. I got this.*

Surfing may have looked easy, but I got totally pummeled that day. I couldn't even make it out to the break because I kept getting tossed and turned by the white water. Battered and bruised, I gave up sooner than I would like to admit.

Because my friends cared, they tried to equip me ahead of time for the challenges that lay before me. When danger is imminent, the loving thing to do is to both warn someone and help equip them for the approaching encounter. If this is true for learning to surf, it is markedly true when it comes to the challenges our students face in trying to navigate today's culture. If we love the youth of this world, we will take seriously the task of equipping them with the necessary tools so they can thrive in their faith.

As we have seen, there are a number of reasons young people choose to disengage with the church. But at its heart, the issue is a matter of worldview. In light of our research and experience, we believe the primary reason Gen Z disconnects from the church is our failure to equip them with a biblical worldview that empowers them to understand and navigate today's culture.

In the previous session, we talked about how important relationships are for building trust with a digital generation. But young people also need a worldview through which they can make sense of information bombardment. In this session, we explore the nature of worldview, unpack some unique worldview challenges we face in equipping this generation, and offer some practical steps for helping young people think and live *Christianly*.

THINK ABOUT THE NEXT GENERATION

1. Try to answer the following questions according to a biblical worldview:

- What is the purpose of human life?
- What kind of life brings genuine happiness?
- What is the basis of morality?
- Does God exist?
- Is there life after death?

2. How would people from other worldviews (or cultures) try to answer these same questions?

WATCH THE VIDEO AND TAKE NOTES

1. Take a minute to guess what percentage of young people today hold the following beliefs. The answers will be provided later in the video:

_____% Believe gender is how a person feels, not their birth sex.

_____% Believe happiness is defined by financial success.

_____% Believe lying is morally wrong.

_____% Believe science and church teachings are complementary.

_____% Believe many religions can lead to eternal life, as there is no one true religion.

2. Studies show that kids who _____ _____ _____ like Jesus does are more likely to _____ like Jesus does.

3. Define *worldview*.

4. Competing worldviews to Christianity:

5. Ways to discover our kids' worldview and to instill a Christian world-view in them:

RESPOND IN YOUR OWN WORDS

1. How well did you do with the Gen Z quiz?

Which statistic surprised you most?

Which statistic do you find the most troubling?

These statistics reflect what Gen Z *believes*. How do you think these issues affect the way that Gen Z *behaves*?

How different do you think these statistics are from your generation?

2. Which of the worldviews mentioned in the video session are you most familiar with?

What other prominent worldviews are you aware of?

IDEAS HAVE CONSEQUENCES

What we believe about the world shapes how we live in the world. There is a connection between our behaviors, our values, our worldview, and our relationships:

- *Behaviors* are simply the choices that we make.
- *Values* inform our behaviors, which are the things we consider important.
- *Worldview* determines what we value.
- Worldviews are primarily shaped and learned through *relationships*.

Name a few things you value most.

How is this list influenced by your Christian worldview?

How do your values shape the way that you live?

RECOGNIZE THE DIFFERENCE BETWEEN COMPETING WORLDVIEWS

In the last session, we considered relational counterfeits. Here are three of the more pressing worldview counterfeits for Gen Z:

Naturalism is the belief that God does not exist and natural forces are sufficient to explain everything. According to naturalism, there is no God, soul, or other supernatural beings.

Pantheism is the belief that *all* is god and distinctions are artificial. Pantheistic beliefs can be seen in modern New Age practices such as channeling and astrology.

Individualism is the view that life is about *me*. The purpose of life is to be authentic to yourself and to live according to your feelings without obligation to anyone or anything beyond the self. Sin involves being inauthentic, and salvation comes from discovering "yourself."

1. What is the unique danger that each of these worldviews presents?

Which worldview do you find the most challenging to engage with?

2. Where have you seen these three worldviews being promoted? Try to give specific examples, like a certain movie or TV show.

3. What do you think makes each of these worldviews appealing to Gen Z?

4. How have you personally noticed these worldviews influencing the young people in your life?

How might youth be unaware of the influences of these counterfeit worldviews?

GROW YOUR OWN WORLDVIEW

If we want to help young people develop a Christian worldview, an important first step is to strengthen our own. Consider the following practical ways to think more deeply about theology, worldview, and apologetics:

- Read a good book(s)
- Watch some videos
- Attend a class at church (or start one)
- Follow worldview experts and apologists on social media
- Listen to a theology, worldview, or apologetics podcast

1. Which of these things are you currently doing to develop your Christian worldview?

2. What classes or seminars in theology, worldview, or apologetics does your church offer?

HELP STUDENTS PRACTICE THEIR FAITH

Equipping students with a biblical worldview is not a matter of mind transformation alone. We do not act simply from what we *believe*, but also from what we *love*. Because love is a virtue that is often learned through practice, by providing young people with experiences, we can help connect their hearts and minds. Some examples include:

- Teach young people the biblical view of poverty, and then take them to serve the poor.
- Whenever you discuss a topic, ask, "So what? How does this affect the way we should live

today?" Make practical connections from biblical truth to relationships.

- Explore God's view of the unborn, and then take your teens to visit a pregnancy resource center to learn about loving and serving women with unplanned pregnancies.

1. Are you already doing this type of activity with your children or students? If so, what are you doing?

2. List some other ways that we can model our Christian worldview alongside young people:

ENGAGE IN WORLDVIEW CONVERSATIONS

This generation needs to know *how* to reason more than to simply learn *what* to think.

This is best done through asking thoughtful questions (and, of course, being a good listener). When you do, keep a few things in mind:

- Resist the urge to give easy answers. Students quickly Google simple responses.
- Ask inquisitive questions that unlock deeper understanding.
- Guide young people to discover truth for themselves.

- Through your body language, words, and actions, be sure young people know you are a safe person to talk to.

1. What are some other ways we can help teach Gen Z how to think well?

What are other methods that you have personally found useful?

Jesus provided His followers with *the* biblical worldview. As the *source* of truth, He understood that His claims affected *every* aspect of reality, and He helped His followers practice what He taught them. Nobody modeled the task of asking thoughtful questions better than He did.

2. What are some of the probing questions Jesus asked during His ministry?

Why do you think Jesus asked so many questions instead of simply preaching and teaching all the time?

PAUSE FOR PERSONAL ASSESSMENT

1. Which of the contending worldviews do you think influences *you* the most?

What is the biggest worldview influencer in your life? TV, social media, etc.

2. When you are in conversation with your peers, do you find yourself listening or talking more?

When you engage with young people, do you find yourself more often lecturing or do you take the time to listen to them and their concerns? If you don't listen well, why not?

3. What was your biggest takeaway from this lesson?

MAKE A PLAN

1. What practical steps can you take to ensure that you have a fully formed Christian worldview?

What resources do you know of to help enrich your Christian worldview?

2. Respond briefly to two questions J. Warner asked in the video:
   Do we know our kids well enough to know what their worldview is?

   Do you have a strategy in place to teach Christian worldview?

3. Now, formulate a game plan in response to those two questions:
   Steps to learn the worldview of the Gen Zers in your life:

Steps to instill a Christian worldview in the next generation:

Based on your role with Gen Z, here are some further suggestions on how to better establish a Christian worldview with a young person:

IF YOU'RE A PARENT
Maximize your mealtime

Parents who regularly share a meal with their children are more likely to pass on their worldview. Here are a few principles and practical tips for mealtimes:

- Have realistic expectations. Roll with unplanned conversations.
- Turn off technology so you can be together without distraction.
- Read a passage of Scripture you have personally been studying or reflecting on.
- Discuss a current event.
- Share a prayer request or answered prayer.

IF YOU'RE A YOUTH PASTOR OR MINISTER
Focus on worldview

In serving as youth pastors, we both have taught biblical worldview through trial and error. Here are some practical ideas we have learned along the way:

- Make regular worldview and apologetics connections in your teaching. Intentionally link biblical truth to your students' lives and relationships.
- Teach a specific unit on worldview. Set aside a predetermined number of weeks to focus on teaching students how to think Christianly (see the appendix of *So the Next Generation Will Know* for an example).
- Here are some teaching strategies we have found helpful:

1. Lecture
2. Discussion
3. YouTube or other videos
4. Guest speaker
5. Offer an equipping seminar for parents

Try not to think of worldview as something you do in addition to your normal ministry with students. Rather, see your ministry as always seeking to fortify students with a Christian worldview so they can live out their faith with clarity and boldness as ambassadors for Christ.

 ### *IF YOU'RE A CHRISTIAN EDUCATOR*
For your students

No matter how "time crunched" you may feel to get through your course's required material, there are still intentional ways to develop a Christian worldview in the classroom:

- Find and share practical ways in which your subject area and the Christian worldview intersect.

- Discuss current events that overlap with your class and the Christian faith.
- Show a movie clip or a YouTube video that makes a connection between your subject and faith.

These efforts do not have to take a lot of class time. It could be as simple as five minutes every Friday at the beginning of class. If you plan these intentionally, you might be surprised how memorable they are and how much they influence your students.

GATHER YOUR THOUGHTS

We are called to build relationships with this generation, but we are also called to "destroy arguments" raised up against the knowledge of God. As we help young people think biblically about all areas of life, they must learn how to reject false ideas that stand in the way of the gospel. But before we can teach Gen Z, we need a fully formed Christian worldview ourselves. Equip yourself first so you can prepare the next generation to repel counterfeit worldviews.

> For though we walk in the flesh, we are not waging war according to the flesh. For the weapons of our warfare are not of the flesh but have divine power to destroy strongholds. We destroy arguments and every lofty opinion raised against the knowledge of God, and take every thought captive to obey Christ. (2 Corinthians 10:3–5)

INCREASE YOUR UNDERSTANDING

To better strengthen the biblical worldview of young people, read *So the Next Generation Will Know*, chapter 4, "Love *Equips*." Take notes specifically on the following sections:

Recognize the Compartmentalization of Faith (page 86):

Recognize the Connection between Faith and Knowledge (page 88):

Session 5

LOVE *IGNITES*
DEVELOPING A PASSION FOR TRUTH

"Ethan, stop arguing with Jim!" shouted John as he sat next to me (J. Warner), preparing the opening statement for perhaps our most publicized homicide trial. Ethan, John's co-prosecutor in the case, was sitting across the table from us. He had abandoned any effort to help John about thirty minutes prior to the outburst. Instead, he was deeply engaged in a conversation with me about the existence of God. Ethan was (and still is) a committed skeptic, passionate about his views and eager to talk with anyone who disagrees with his commitment to atheism.

"Jim loves it when you ask all these questions," continued John. "He'll talk to you about this *all day long*, and if you keep this up, we're never going to get anything done. You need to be more like *me*. Jim knows *I don't care* about any of this God stuff. That's why we don't waste any time talking about it."

John was right. In the nearly twenty years I have worked with him, he's the least interested person I know. It's been difficult to talk with him about God or Christianity. He's not pretending, either; he truly *doesn't care*, and his apathy has paralyzed our conversations. But

John is one of my dearest friends. I love him like a brother, and I can't imagine living in eternity without him.

Maybe you've had a similar experience with someone *you* love. If you're investing in the lives of young people, you've almost certainly experienced the paralysis of apathy. As a youth pastor, I almost always had someone in our group who appeared disinterested. It's difficult to teach the truth to young people you love when they aren't really listening. But that didn't stop me. Because I loved my students, I wanted them to become passionate believers.

So how can we help young, spiritually dispassionate Christians avoid the apathy of John and the atheistic passion of Ethan?

THINK ABOUT THE NEXT GENERATION

1. List a few things you think this generation is passionate about.

2. Can you think of any young people in your life who aren't interested in spiritual things? What types of spiritual subjects have you tried to engage them in?

WATCH THE VIDEO AND TAKE NOTES

1. The biggest threat to theism is not atheism but _____.

2. What are the barriers standing between young people and a passionate faith?

3. We need to give young people two _____ for every _____.

4. The two "whys":

RESPOND IN YOUR OWN WORDS

Was there a time in your life when you placed less importance on spiritual things?

What were you focusing on instead?

What was it that shook you out of your apathy?

How can you use this experience to help reach young people who may be in the same spiritual state?

TWO "WHYS" FOR EVERY "WHAT"

As parents, pastors, and educators, we've all explained what is true to our young people. But simple propositions about the nature of God or the claims of Christianity may or may not ignite a fire in our young people. That's why we suggest taking two additional steps. For every *what* you offer the young people in your life, be sure to add two *whys*.

Let's practice. The following are some issues related to Christian theology, apologetics, and culture:

- God's creation of the universe
- The resurrection of Jesus
- Human sexuality

First answer the "what," the biblical stance of the issue. Then take some time and answer the two "whys":

1. *Why* is the biblical view true? What supporting evidence is there inside and outside of the Bible?
2. *Why* does it matter? Try to think about current cultural topics that are connected to this biblical issue. Each biblical issue may have more far-reaching impacts on cultural issues than are immediately obvious to you as well as to Gen Z, so really spend time on this question in particular.

PASSION-BUILDING PRINCIPLES

One way to help spark a passionate faith in young people is to remove obstacles preventing it.

1. List the obstacles:

Which obstacle has the potential to keep *you* from a fuller, more passionate faith?

Which one do you think is the greatest obstacle to the young people in your life?

Let's examine a few simple *passion-building* principles that can help you set the stage for your interactions with young people (more are listed in the *So the Next Generation Will Know* book):

Model Passion

Let your passion for God *overflow* in front of your kids. Become the kind of teacher, leader, or parent your young believers can model.

Raise Expectations

In many Christian youth groups, the emphasis is more on friendship and fun. If that's all we are offering, why would we be surprised when our students eventually seek other alternatives? Instead, let's elevate our expectations and allow God's Spirit to ignite a passion.

Stay Relevant

If we want our young people to be passionate about the things of God, we need to make sure we show them *why* our claims are true, and *why* they matter in the first place.

Do Something

Provide young Christians with an opportunity to put truth into *action*. Honor their restlessness by creating activities and opportunities that bring claims about God and Christianity to life.

2. Which of the passion-building principles listed are you currently employing with young people?

Which ones do you think would make the greatest impact with your young people?

3. Reflect on your church's youth group. Is it just some form of wholesome entertainment, or are the young people being challenged?

If they aren't being challenged, what are some ways that your church can raise the bar for them?

4. Look back to your list of things that young people are passionate about from the Think about the Next Generation section. How can you tap into these passions to help your young people cultivate a greater passion for things of faith?

5. What opportunities are there in your neighborhood to help put your young people's faith into action?

THE IMPORTANCE OF COMMUNITY

The earliest followers of Jesus "were continually devoting themselves to the apostles' teaching" (Acts 2:42 NASB). When a community reads God's Word and gathers together, God uses the enthusiasm of more passionate believers to elevate the interest of those who might otherwise be less energized.

Was there a specific worship service or Bible study that helped ignite *your* passion for Christianity?

What was it about that meeting that impacted you so greatly?

How can you replicate this with the young people you come into contact with?

PAUSE FOR PERSONAL ASSESSMENT

1. How often do you pray for this generation?

2. Have you ever assumed that a young person was apathetic toward Christianity as an excuse to not engage with that person?

3. How are you showing your passion for Christianity to the next generation?

4. Two of the obstacles to passionate Christianity mentioned in this session are personal sin and misplaced priorities. Take time and reflect on any issues in your own life. You don't need to share them with the group, but write them down to personally acknowledge them.

5. If someone were to ask you right now why you think Christianity is true, how would you respond?

6. What was your biggest takeaway from this lesson?

MAKE A PLAN

1. Which one or two passion-building principles can you put into action this week with the young people in your life?

2. What practical steps can you take to improve your own passion for Christianity?

3. Continue practicing *"two whys for every what"* throughout the week. List two or three issues here that you want to explore, as well as the "what" explanation according to the Christian worldview. By next week, answer two "why" questions for each issue.

4. Identify a young person in your life who is passionate about Christianity. Make it a point to connect with him or her this week. Try to identify:

Why this person is so passionate about Christianity.

What positive Christian influences or mentors this person has.

How can you leverage this one person's experience to help other young people become more passionate about Christianity?

Based on your role with Gen Z, here are some further suggestions on how to better ignite a passion for truth within young people:

IF YOU'RE A PARENT
"Two whys for every what" in family life

You don't have to wait for a scheduled family gathering to teach "two whys for every what." When you hear a claim on the radio, in a movie or video, or just around the dinner table, help your kids define the claim (the "what"), ask them if they think there is any evidence to support the claim (the first "why"), then ask them why the issue matters (the second "why").

IF YOU'RE A YOUTH PASTOR OR MINISTER
"Two whys for every what" in your messages

Imagine preaching through the gospel of John, starting in chapter 1: "In the beginning was the Word, and the Word was with God ..."

Important claims in this verse provide opportunities to answer potential questions:

- Why do we believe Jesus is the Word?
- Why do we believe in one triune God rather than two (or three) different Gods?
- Why should we believe that Jesus is God?

In every message, anticipate and address potential "why" questions as you describe what the Bible says in each verse.

Your students are probably aware of the cultural views related to purpose, identity, and value, given their exposure to the internet. Examine these claims from a biblical perspective. Help your students understand why the claims described in the Bible matter.

IF YOU'RE A CHRISTIAN EDUCATOR
"Two whys for every what" in your lessons

If you teach in a Christian school setting, you're probably already telling your students about the claims of the Bible ("what" is true) and perhaps providing them with evidence to support these claims ("why" it's true).

If you're still seeing disinterested students, try spending more time talking about why it matters. Provide a second "why" for every "what." Questions to consider:

- How does this truth impact your own identity as a person? Does it help you see your role in the world? Does it change the way you think about your purpose in life?
- How does this truth change the way you see your friends and family? Does it cause you to be more (or less) patient, compassionate, or understanding?
- How does the Christian view differ from alternative views on this topic? Why does the Christian claim do a better job explaining reality than any of the alternatives?
- If we made a list, comparing the Christian claim with its alternatives, what are the strengths and weaknesses of each claim? How does each claim impact our lives and the world around us?

Allow these questions to guide your preparation, and be sure to include the reason why Christianity matters as you teach its principles and doctrines.

GATHER YOUR THOUGHTS

When you're truly passionate about something, you want everyone else to be passionate about it too. We shouldn't be content with young people merely attending church week after week. We want them to be deeply passionate about their faith in Jesus Christ. But that won't just happen in isolation. We need to model a passionate faith to them and help to remove any obstacles standing in their way.

> Hear, O Israel: The LORD our God, the LORD is one. You shall love the LORD your God with all your heart and with all your soul and with all your might. And these words that I command you today shall be on your heart. You shall teach them diligently to your children, and shall talk of them when you sit in your house, and when you walk by the way, and when you lie down, and when you rise. (Deuteronomy 6:4–7)

INCREASE YOUR UNDERSTANDING

To better understand *additional* strategies to ignite passion in Gen Z, read *So the Next Generation Will Know*, chapter 5, "Love *Ignites*." Take notes on the following additional strategies:

Seek God:

Recognize Diversity:

Cultivate Relationships:

Define Truth:

Take a Long-Term Perspective:

Session 6

LOVE *TRAINS*
RESISTING THE DESIRE TO ENTERTAIN RATHER THAN TRAIN

"Jim, can Joey and I meet with you?"

I (J. Warner) immediately felt some trepidation about the request. Joey's dad sounded serious over the phone, and I could hear his voice quiver as he described the problem to me. Joey was slowly slipping away from our youth group, from his family, and from his commitment to Jesus. He was bright, friendly, and engaging. But he had been hanging out with friends who introduced him to drugs at an early age.

Joey was a part of our youth group before I became the pastor, and he had been an active member for several years. During my first year, he was one of the students I worried about most. He was attracted to the activities we hosted, and like many other youth groups in Southern California, our calendar was filled with camps and outings involving board sports of one kind or another. Spring wakeboarding. Summer surf camp. Winter snowboarding. At each of these events, we managed to slip in a Christian message at the end of the day, but if I'm honest, that wasn't our true focus. Far more time was spent *entertaining* our students (and their friends) than *teaching* or *training* them as Christian believers.

Now, after only a year as Joey's pastor, I couldn't help but wonder if our priorities as a youth group were misguided. Could we have changed the trajectory of Joey's life? Maybe. Maybe not. But his situation highlighted an imbalance in our engagement with the students. We were more focused on mirroring the priorities of our culture than igniting a passion for God. Joey's story was just another motivation for me to redesign our approach and move from *entertaining* to *training*.

THINK ABOUT THE NEXT GENERATION

1. Have you ever had a similar situation with a young person? If so, how did you react to it?

What could you have done better to prevent it?

2. What is the difference between entertaining and training?

In what ways do you challenge your kids to do more than just surface-level activities?

WATCH THE VIDEO AND TAKE NOTES

1. What is the difference between teaching and training? How does the purpose of each differ?

2. What does the acronym TRAIN stand for?

> T_____
> R_____
> A_____
> I_____
> N_____

3. What does the acronym TAB stand for?

> T_____
> A_____
> B_____

RESPOND IN YOUR OWN WORDS

Training is *teaching toward a challenge*. The simple TRAIN acronym describes the training process used with students:

T – Test: Challenge students to expose weaknesses

Young people are shown how much they *don't* know by exposing them to the objections of nonbelievers or alternate views from differing religions.

R – Require: Expect more from students

Raise the expectations for each student, offering this elevated expectation as a sign of respect. In other words, treat them as responsible adults, ready and capable to take on the challenges that will be scheduled for them.

A – Arm: Teach students the truth so they can defend it

Next, carefully examine the claims of Christianity in light of the common objections offered. This takes time and it is specifically targeted at the challenge students are being asked to accept.

I – Involve: Deploy students into the battlefield of ideas

Craft a challenge for your students and set it on the calendar. The entire training process is pointed toward this challenge. The culminating event is designed to motivate students to attend and participate, giving the teaching a sense of importance and urgency as the date approaches.

N – Nurture: Tend to the wounds students may suffer, and model the nature of Jesus

Finally, prepare for the inevitable "bumps and bruises" students will suffer as they encounter people who oppose Christianity and resist their efforts to share the truth. You can draw on the "capital" of your relationships *if* you've invested in your young people prior to difficult times.

1. Which areas of the TRAIN process are you and your young people actively engaging in?

Which areas have you been neglecting?

Which area do you think your young people hesitate to participate in?

Why do you think the "nurture" aspect is so important?

2. What are some appropriate challenges for your young people, given their current level of training?

TAB WORLDVIEW TRAINING
Theology (Doctrine)

Begin by describing *what* is true. Young people need to know what the Bible teaches, especially at a time when most Christians don't. Theology obliges Christians to discuss the nature and role of

Scripture; the attributes of God, Jesus, and the Holy Spirit; the definition of salvation; the nature of humans; and the role of the church.

1. From your experience, which aspects of Christian theology are most misunderstood by young people?

Why do you think this is the case?

What specific external influences contribute to this?

Apologetics (Defense)

For every theological claim you make to your youth, you must answer this critical *why* question. Young people eagerly want to know if Christianity can be *defended*. Take small steps toward preparing yourself to address issues related to truth, God's existence, the reliability of the Bible, Christianity, and alternative worldviews.

2. Which of these apologetics categories do *you* struggle with most?

3. From your experience, which categories do your *young people* struggle with most?

If the categories you and your young people struggle with are different, why do you think this is the case?

Behavior (Demeanor and Deeds)

Help young people understand how the claims of Christianity impact their lives. Theology and apologetics are not directionless pursuits. They point toward holy behaviors and provide answers to several questions that matter to young people:

Who Am I?

Young people often define their identity in destructive or unproductive behaviors. But these fleeting approaches fail to provide young people with a meaningful identity. Our status and distinctiveness in Christ, on the other hand, provide us with a transcendent, *lasting* identity.

What Is My Purpose?

Our identity is linked closely to our sense of purpose, and young people want an answer to the question: "Why am I here?" Youth, like many of their older peers, seek to find purpose in work, recreation, and relationships.

How Should I Live?
God's Word provides guidance and protection to those who "walk in the same way in which Jesus walked." Scripture helps every believer navigate the world in which we live. It guides us toward loving, healthy responses and protects us from dangerous, destructive choices.

4. Why is the "Who am I?" question so important for young people?

5. Where are the young people in your lives seeking to find their purpose?

6. In your church, which aspect of TAB do the parents of students most want emphasized?

Why do you think this is the case?

How do theology and apologetics empower the behavior aspect?

HOW, EXACTLY, SHOULD WE TRAIN?

Now that we've described the *content* of our training, let's take a brief look at a number of simple training imperatives:

Be Persistent

Don't assume that one spiritual discussion, lecture, or sermon will be enough to engrain truth into the minds of young people. Revisit theological, apologetic, and behavioral topics *repeatedly*.

Be Balanced

Remember that two "whys" for every "what" requires *balance* in conversations and instruction. When conversations get out of balance and lean too heavily on one of these three legs, they may sound lopsided or preachy.

Be Practical

Because of how deep-seated secularism is in the culture, students often do *not* make natural connections from their beliefs to their behavior. That's why it's important to regularly help them see how theology shapes their actions.

Be Personal and Contextual

Look for available curriculums, online syllabuses, internet resources (and even the TAB outline we've given you in this session) as a *starting point.* Use this material to form and supplement your own material. Become a dedicated student, and take the time to modify existing plans and curriculums to meet your specific needs.

Be Adventurous

Training isn't training unless it's preparation for a real challenge. As you provide two "whys" for every "what," point your training toward something *adventurous*. Young people have always been drawn to edgy experiences. Let's create some that will give them confidence that Christianity is true. More on this in the next session.

1. In which training imperative are you strongest?

In which one are you weakest?

2. Which training imperative(s) do you think your group of young people will value most?

PAUSE FOR PERSONAL ASSESSMENT

1. Do you feel you have been properly trained to defend the Christian faith?

Which aspect do you think your church body overlooks as a whole?

Which aspect is your church excelling at?

2. Which aspects of TAB worldview training do you feel are your strengths, and which do you think you are lacking?

MAKE A PLAN

1. What steps can you take to ensure that *you* are being trained in your Christian faith?

What people or groups in your church or community exist to help equip each other? If none exists, consider starting your own!

2. Training the next generation requires time, planning, and dedication. What small steps can you take this week to begin the process? Be as specific as possible.

3. Set some concrete training goals for your young people. What types of challenges would you like them to handle one month from now? Six months? One year?

4. What was your biggest takeaway from this lesson?

Based on your role with Gen Z, here are some further suggestions on how to TRAIN young people:

 IF YOU'RE A PARENT
Take advantage of TAB opportunities
The TAB training model, based on theology, apologetics, and behavior, encourages you to initiate conversations with your kids by allowing one of these three categories to act as a catalyst. Here are a few examples:

- When a loved one dies, or something bad happens to a friend or family member, use the opportunity

to discuss Christian theology related to the after-life or to the problem of evil.
- When someone in a movie or on television treats Mohammed, Buddha, or Jesus as if they were just religious leaders, talk about the evidence for Jesus' divinity or the evidence for the resurrection.
- When a friend gets in trouble at school, talk about how behaviors are tied to worldviews and why the Christian worldview can guide and protect us.

In each of these cases, allow the theological, apologetic, or behavioral catalyst to start the conversation, but make sure you include all three categories (and two "whys" for every "what") in your discussion. Make sure your kids connect that our theological foundations can be supported evidentially and ultimately result in behaviors that help us understand our role in the world.

IF YOU'RE A YOUTH PASTOR OR MINISTER
Create some series
When I (J. Warner) served as a youth pastor, I charted a scope of curriculums that would allow me to teach all three TAB training elements to my students. Here are some examples:

- **The Sacred Life** – a six-week theology series based on the Apostles' Creed
- **Living above the Lies** – an eight-week apologetics series based on the eight most common objec-tions to Christianity
- **My Life Lived His Way** – a six-week series based on six common behavioral struggles for teens

You can create similar series by using reliable sources on the internet to research each topic (see the appendix of *So the Next Generation Will Know*). As you are teaching through one of the three TAB topics, be sure to include two "whys" for every "what," connecting the dots between theology, apologetics, and behavior.

IF YOU'RE A CHRISTIAN EDUCATOR
Don't wait

One of the most important steps for Christian educators to effectively train students is to have a scope and sequence that unfolds logically and naturally. For instance, I (Sean) developed this four-year Bible curriculum for each grade in high school when I was the department chair:

> **9th:** Old Testament Survey
> **10th:** New Testament Survey
> **11th:** Systematic Theology, Cults, and Comparative Religions
> **12th:** Apologetics and Worldview

Given that many Gen Zers encounter skepticism as early as the elementary years, it is vital to teach apologetics and theology early and consistently. Reserving apologetics for senior Bible is often too late. Don't assume your students have an adequate understanding of the Bible or how to defend it.

GATHER YOUR THOUGHTS

Depending on how long you have been a Christian, you have probably heard countless sermons and attended many Bible studies. But it is not enough to simply be taught; we must train. The same goes for the next generation. Our culture is getting more hostile toward Christianity, and if the church experience of our young people only consists of pizza, basketball, and a light message, their faith is not going to survive long. If you truly love the next generation, you need to train them for the challenges they are going to face.

> Train up a child in the way he should go; even when he is old he will not depart from it. (Proverbs 22:6)

INCREASE YOUR UNDERSTANDING

This session is based on *So the Next Generation Will Know*, chapter 6, "Love *Trains*." Review the TAB Training model (on pages 124–32), focusing on the Apologetics (Defense) section. Take notes for the following areas of inquiry to identify the important questions you may need to study so you can teach these topics to the young people in your life:

Issues Related to Truth:

Issues Related to God's Existence:

Issues Related to the Bible:

Issues Related to Christianity:

Issues Related to Jesus:

Issues Related to Alternative Christian Views:

Issues Related to Alternative Worldviews:

Issues Related to Ethics:

Session 7

LOVE *EXPLORES*
PROVIDING LIFE-CHANGING ADVENTURES FOR STUDENTS

"Pastor Jim?" asked Daniel as he finished a slice of pizza and watched the college students walk back and forth along Telegraph Avenue. "Do you think we'll ever do another wakeboarding trip?" I (J. Warner) smiled and looked at my good friend Brett Kunkle,[3] who was sitting next to me. He started to laugh.

Years earlier I asked Brett to speak at our high school summer camp, one of many board-sport trips our church took in the early months of my ministry. Brett introduced our group to Christian apologetics during that memorable week, and he helped me recalibrate our youth ministry over the next two years.

"Well," I replied to Daniel, "we could definitely add a wakeboarding trip to our calendar, but it would require us to cancel one of these mission trips ..." I paused. Daniel looked thoughtful. Brett and I waited for his response.

"Never mind then," he said succinctly and then continued eating.

As fun as our board-sport camps had been, they really couldn't compare to the TAB training missions that had become a part of our ethos as a group. Daniel had been part of a twenty-five-student team who had just spent the afternoon on the Campus of UC Berkeley. We had been sharing the truth of Christianity with students on the campus, and although our students were much younger than their university counterparts, they were equipped and prepared, exploring their faith as Christians in a way that grew both their knowledge *and* their confidence.

Many of these students would tell stories about these trips for years to come. Most would say they were *transformational*. Our Berkeley mission trip was one of several challenges we calendared to turn *teaching* into *training*. These TAB trips were designed to take advantage of our students' adventurous natures and create an environment where young believers could explore their faith and *thrive*.

And they were more popular than *anything* else we did as a group.

THINK ABOUT THE NEXT GENERATION

If you attended a youth group when you were younger, what were the most memorable activities?

What was their purpose?

How prepared do you think your current group of young people is to engage people of different worldviews?

WATCH THE VIDEO AND TAKE NOTES

1. What are the ways that we can challenge our young people?

2. What are simple ways to inoculate the next generation?

RESPOND IN YOUR OWN WORDS

1. How would you feel about sending your young people on a worldview trip? Would you be hesitant and afraid, or would you be excited at the opportunity for spiritual growth?

2. Does a drastic change in perspective seem out of reach for your group of young people? Why or why not?

3. Why is it important to calendar a challenge?

IMAGINING THE CHALLENGE

TAB training comes to life when you schedule a deployment. This single act, of calendaring a challenge, turns teaching into training. Let the following brief list of suggestions become your starting point (for more ideas, refer to the Increase Your Understanding section near the end of this session):

Evangelism (One Afternoon)

Fear is probably the one thing that keeps people from evangelizing in the first place. We've used public evangelism opportunities to form the basis for several weeks of training related to theological issues, apologetics, and behavioral issues.

Teaching in a Family or Class Setting (One Afternoon)

One of the best ways to *learn* something is to *teach* it. Ask your kids to teach during your family devotional. If you teach high school Bible at a Christian school, have your students teach a theological or apologetics lesson to younger kids at the school.

Creating a YouTube Video or Blog Entry (One Afternoon)

Create a YouTube channel or simple blog (there are a number of free blog-hosting sites), and ask your students to answer a simple theological or apologetics question on video or in a written format.

Visiting a Local University Campus (One Afternoon or Full Day)

Pick a local university and ask to visit the campus during an academic session so students will be present in the courtyards and common spaces. If possible, arrange a meeting with a student group (either Christian, religious, or atheist) to talk about spiritual matters, or simply ask what life on the campus is like, given their worldview.

Visiting a Religious Community or Facility (One Afternoon or Full Day)

Students who attend these opportunities are challenged to learn how to respond in love, even when someone makes a false claim about Christianity. Exhibiting solid behavioral training prior to these trips is crucial.

Taking a TAB Trip (Three to Seven Days)

These deployments occur over several days and nights and are more intensive than anything else we've described so far, but that's what makes them so *transformational*. We've taken several trips of this nature in the following TAB categories:

Theological TAB Trips

Theological TAB trips involve three to seven days at a location in your region that has a high concentration of believers from a religion *other* than Christianity. We've taken our students to Salt Lake City to engage Mormon believers, and to areas in Los Angeles County that have high Muslim populations.

Apologetics TAB Trips

Apologetics TAB trips require three to seven days on a secular university campus in your region. We chose the University of California at Berkeley, an aggressively secular campus.

Behavioral TAB Trips

Behavioral TAB trips involve one to two days helping in ministries that serve the poor, homeless, needy, and addicted. We decided to partner with local ministries for our behavioral trips because we wanted our youth to develop relationships they could continue long after the trip was over.

Think about your group of young people and your community. Which short-term challenge do you think they are most prepared to face right now? Why?

Which long-term TAB trip do you think would most benefit your group? Why?

While all these activities are useful in creating the kind of deployment opportunities that transform teaching into training, the three- to seven-day TAB trips are *by far* the most effective. We'll spend the rest of this lesson trying to help you make these kinds of trips a real possibility for your family, youth group, or class.

SETTING THE CHALLENGE

Begin by establishing the kind of trip you want to lead (related to your efforts to teach theology, apologetics, or behavior). Then determine the date and location for your trip:

Pick a Location

Do some research to see if there is a university, religious community, or service ministry that matches your needs and is within driving distance of your home, church, or school.

Find a Few Partners

Next, start exploring potential partners to help you host and train your students. You'll need a location that provides sleeping quarters, a kitchen, and a place to meet as a group. Look for a local church.

Build Your Team

Longer TAB trips require a dedicated volunteer team. If possible, include one adult for every four to five students. The majority of these adult leaders should attend all the training sessions for the trip, because you'll need them to help answer questions and counsel students.

Set a Date

As you consider setting the date for one of these trips, think about the events you might want to engage in the city you'll be visiting. Also, contemplate how you can weave these trips into your teaching calendar, remembering that every trip is preceded by weeks of training.

1. List the universities, religious communities, and service ministries within a reasonable distance of your church.

2. List some people you think would be good team members and what role they would be best suited for.

3. When does your youth group or school have free time in its calendar to schedule a trip?

PREPARING FOR THE CHALLENGE

Once the training begins, tell students you want to *raise the bar*. Start by role-playing as an atheist or someone from a different religious or belief system. Push your students in order to reveal their weaknesses in answering simple objections or refuting alternate claims. Then reveal your plan to help them become better case makers by taking them on an adventure unlike anything they've ever experienced before.

Next, pick and assign a reading text. For our Berkeley trip, we used *I Don't Have Enough Faith to Be an Atheist* by Norman Geisler and Frank Turek. Using the chapter structure of this book as an outline, we established a training schedule and required students to be present for at least six of the eight training sessions if they wanted to go on the trip.

Training sessions can take place during your weekly meeting if you're a youth pastor, during your class time if you're an educator, or once a week during your family devotional.

1. List some acquaintances who do not share a Christian worldview that you could have speak with your group of young people.

2. List some resources that would serve as good training materials. (To find more, see the appendix of *So the Next Generation Will Know*.)

3. Everyone has a busy schedule, but remember the subject of our first lesson: love sacrifices. What time(s) do you have available to train your young people?

PAUSE FOR PERSONAL ASSESSMENT

1. How equipped do you think *you* are to face one of the challenges listed in this session?

2. Would you have been prepared for this type of challenge as a teen? Why or why not?

3. What was your biggest takeaway from this lesson?

MAKE A PLAN

1. Look over the list of challenges. Pick one that would be best suitable for your group of young people.

2. Check your calendar.

Set a date for the challenge.

Set regular days and times for training.

3. Establish your training curriculum. (See the appendix of *So the Next Generation Will Know* for resources.)

4. Build your team. Over the next week, find some people who will partner with you for the challenge.

5. Aside from the "big challenge," find one or two simple ways to begin inoculating the young people in your life. Examples: watching and discussing YouTube videos or studying an apologetics book together.

Based on your role with Gen Z, here are some further suggestions on how to challenge your young people:

IF YOU'RE A PARENT
Find a way to take a worldview mission trip

But what if your youth group or Christian school doesn't understand their value? Here are a few suggestions:

- Do your best to explain the value of these trips to the pastors and Christian educators who lead and teach your students.
- Prepare yourself and offer to role-play as an atheist or non-Christian to demonstrate the need for training to your pastor or teacher. Or find someone who can do it.
- Offer to host training meetings, or help lead, train, or escort the students who participate in the trip.
- Consider partnering with a group of like-minded parents to take a trip. The principles and guidelines we offer in this session will help you lead your own trip.

IF YOU'RE A YOUTH PASTOR OR MINISTER
Take "baby steps"

A TAB trip is probably a new idea for most youth pastors. Start small, using some of the suggestions we've offered in this session. Consider forming and taking trips in the following order:

- Take your students for an afternoon conducting spiritual surveys at a local shopping center.

- Arrange a visit at a local university for a day to conduct surveys and meet with a student group to talk about issues of faith.
- Arrange a visit at a local Mormon ward, Muslim mosque, or other religious facility to take a tour and engage leaders with questions.

Use shorter TAB excursions to pave the way for longer trips and experiences.

IF YOU'RE A CHRISTIAN EDUCATOR
Get some help

If you would like to add a TAB trip to your calendar but are concerned about the logistics involved, we have a few suggestions:

- First, examine your school calendar to see if there is something you could replace with a TAB trip—if only for a year on a trial basis. See if your leadership is willing to use the resources and volunteers they would typically use for another mission trip for a TAB trip.
- Second, delegate. We started by partnering with Brett Kunkle at MavenTruth.com. He's developed a system that will help you get started and eventually equip you to lead trips on your own. Find a champion on your campus, such as a Bible teacher or chaplain, and connect him or her with Brett.
- Finally, start small with a local three-day trip, and work your way up to a five-day trip in another

region. It's easier to correct mistakes when you're close to home.

Do what it takes to shift your efforts toward a more comprehensive approach that culminates in a learning adventure your students will never forget.

GATHER YOUR THOUGHTS

We cannot shelter our young people their entire lives. They need to learn how to face the various challenges to their faith. That's why we need to be the ones to challenge them in the context of a safe Christian environment. By inoculating our young people as early as possible, they can grow to become mature, passionate followers of Christ.

> See to it that no one takes you captive by philosophy and empty deceit, according to human tradition, according to the elemental spirits of the world, and not according to Christ. (Colossians 2:8)

INCREASE YOUR UNDERSTANDING

There are more ideas for challenges in *So the Next Generation Will Know*, chapter 7, "Love *Explores*." Focus specifically on the Surveys and Conversations section on pages 141–42 and the example of a Spiritual Survey offered in the appendix on pages 186–87:

Surveys and Conversations:
Why is this approach one of the easiest ways to "deploy"?

Example of Spiritual Survey:

Which of these questions do you think will be the most useful in generating conversations?

If you could change one question to better suit your young people or the context of your setting, what new question would you add?

Session 8

LOVE *ENGAGES*
PREPARING STUDENTS THROUGH MOVIES, MUSIC, SOCIAL MEDIA, AND CURRENT EVENTS

In high school, my parents took me (Sean), my older sister, and my girlfriend to see the Holocaust movie *Schindler's List*. You might be thinking, *That's crazy. Why would your parents take you to see an R-rated movie with sexuality and graphic violence?* The answer is because my parents saw it as an opportunity to help me think deeply about the historical and philosophical issues raised by the film. When the movie was done, we discussed it for two hours over dinner. To this day, I still remember much of our conversation.

My parents were modeling an important point: *love teaches kids to thoughtfully and confidently engage the world around them.* When I was in high school in the early '90s, cultural messages came primarily through movies, television, and music. These mediums are still powerful today, but since Gen Zers are the first truly digital generation, we must also teach them how to thoughtfully engage the world of smartphones and social media.

My (Sean's) son didn't get a smartphone until he was fourteen and a half. My (J. Warner's) daughters didn't get phones until their junior and senior years in high school. Why so late, by cultural standards? The first reason is that we wanted to protect them from potential dangers to their emotional, relational, and psychological health.

But secondly, and more importantly, we saw it as an opportunity to help them learn certain life lessons about responsibility and delayed gratification *before* they got a phone. If you give your son or daughter a phone, or access to social media, too early, you miss a critical opportunity to help prepare them for adulthood.

If we give our kids a phone too early, or promise them one at a certain age, we lose the ability to motivate them toward responsibility and character. How will they understand the power of a phone if we don't require them to demonstrate a certain level of maturity before getting one? And if we don't teach them how to use it properly, how can we expect them not to abuse it?

THINK ABOUT THE NEXT GENERATION

1. When you saw movies as a teen, did you ever have someone to discuss them with afterward?

Would you have been open to it? If so, what would that have meant to you?

2. If you have kids of your own, at what age did you allow them to have their first smartphone?

How did you decide when they were ready to have one?

Do you think it was a good decision, or do you wish you had waited longer? Why?

3. What do you think is the strongest influencer of Gen Z?

What do you think are the most destructive influencers?

4. If you had to rank your level of influence on the young people in your life from 1 to 10 (1 being the least amount of influence and 10 being the greatest level of influence), what would it be? Why?

WATCH THE VIDEO AND TAKE NOTES

1. What is meant by an "opportunity mind-set?"

2. How is this best accomplished?

3. How can we avoid confrontation in our teaching moments with young people?

4. What can we learn from an unsuccessful interaction with our kids?

RESPOND IN YOUR OWN WORDS

1. How would you react if your son or daughter asked to see a movie with questionable content?

Are you inclined to automatically say no, or are you willing to use it as a learning opportunity?

2. How can you integrate teachable moments into your daily routines with your kids?

In order to help young people understand the way media impacts the way we think, we must protect them from *negative* media messages:

Engage Kids Early

Start the conversation with your kids at home before they are confronted with the issues elsewhere. We need to inoculate them with a biblical perspective *before* they are confronted with unbiblical ideas elsewhere.

Model Healthy Technology Use

Before we criticize youth for their digital reliance, we should take an honest look at our own habits. Ask: Do I constantly check social media? Do I feel the need to respond to every text immediately? Do I have my phone out during meals? Do I text while I drive? Can I spend stress-free time away from my phone?

Set Healthy Boundaries for Kids

As kids get older, they should earn more privileges. This prepares them to make wise decisions when they are no longer under our authority. If kids are given privileges before they have demonstrated sufficient responsibility, they will not value them and may abuse them.

1. What *nonconfrontational* questions can you ask your kids about the media they consume that will help them think biblically about it?

2. How can you model healthy technology use to your kids?

What boundaries have you set for *yourself*?

If you responded "none," what boundaries can you set for the sake of your kids? Remember: *love sacrifices*.

3. What technology boundaries have you currently set with your kids?

If you haven't set any, list some ways that you can implement boundaries with your kids to teach them responsibility.

Now let's discuss active ways to use media as an opportunity to teach kids how to engage the world as Christians.

WORLDVIEW AS A NARRATIVE

Worldview is defined as a view of the world that answers three critical questions: (1) How did we get here?—*Origin*; (2) Why is everything so messed up?—*Predicament*; and (3) How can we fix it?—*Resolution*. Here are two examples of alternative worldviews that offer their own explanation of reality:

- *Naturalism* says the world is a cosmic accident (origin), humans have messed things up (predicament), and we must solve our own problems (resolution). Naturalism is often portrayed in YouTube videos, memes, songs, and other forms of modern media.
- *Pantheism* says humans are eternally part of the divine (origin), but that we forgot our godhood (predicament), and need to be reminded so we can become one with the universe (resolution).

1. Can you list a movie or TV show that promotes a specific worldview?

How does it portray the three components of origin, predicament, and resolution?

What are the redeeming aspects of this movie or show?

Are there any ways that it portrays biblical truth?

2. How can you get your young people to examine media through a worldview lens?

What questions can you teach them to ask *themselves* of the media they consume?

THE OPPORTUNITY MIND-SET

Because our world is so media saturated, there are endless opportunities to help young people think biblically. Seize opportunities that naturally arise throughout the course of the day to remind your kids of biblical truth. Here are a few opportunities to consider:

YouTube Videos

YouTube is the search engine of choice for Gen Zers, who watch it for information *and* for entertainment. Given how much they engage with the platform, it is vital we invite them to reflect on how it may influence them and their peers.

Article or Blog from a Skeptic

One of the best ways to engage students is by reading an article or blog from a skeptic. This may pique their interest because it comes from a hostile perspective. Doing this shows confidence in our Christian position and that we are not afraid of a challenge.

Current Events

Daily news events are a wonderful opportunity to help students understand and get involved with culture. Since there is a Christian perspective on *everything*, we can engage students on a number of different kinds of stories: politics, sports, ethics, comparative religions, and more.

1. Do you currently engage in one of these activities with your kids? If so, describe a typical interaction, listing specific questions or comments you may normally raise.

2. What other opportunities are available to help engage students to think wisely about their media use?

At times you may be able to engage in lengthier discussions. Sometimes you may have just a few moments. We suggest not trying to make *everything* spiritual and avoid forcing an unnatural discussion. On the other hand, don't underestimate the power of a good exchange with a young person and the doors it may open in the future. We aim to have this kind of dialogue regularly with young people and hope you will too.

PAUSE FOR PERSONAL ASSESSMENT

1. With which form of media are you *most* familiar?

2. With which form of media are you *least* familiar?

3. How might you improve your familiarity with pop culture and media to better engage the young people in your life?

4. Have you ever blown a perfect opportunity for a teachable moment with a young person?

    If so, what did you learn from it?

Or, do you remember an adult blowing it with you when you were young? What happened?

5. What was your biggest takeaway from this lesson?

MAKE A PLAN

1. Brainstorm a list of movies and TV shows you can use to teach young people about worldview.

Schedule a night this week to watch one of these shows with a young person and to have a meaningful discussion afterward.

2. List some worldview questions that you will regularly raise about the media you and your family consume.

3. Write down one activity from the Opportunity Mind-Set section (earlier in this session) in which you will engage a young person this week.

4. Make a list of some household guidelines and boundaries regarding technology and media use that you will implement with your family (yourself included) this week.

How will you explain this to your family so they understand *why* these guidelines and boundaries are important?

Based on your role with Gen Z, here are some further suggestions on how to engage media thoughtfully and to explore worldview:

IF YOU'RE A PARENT
Have a summer movie extravaganza

Recently I (Sean) came up with a plan to help my older kids engage media more thoughtfully. During summertime, we watched a number of different movies and discussed them as a family. Here are some things I did to make the time meaningful:

- I picked films that were both interesting and had themes we wanted to discuss with our kids. For instance, we watched *42*, which is the story of Jackie Robinson, and then discussed race relations.
- Watch both recent and older films. My kids thoroughly enjoyed *The Elephant Man* (1980), which is filmed in black and white. It raised great questions about human dignity, and they could see how filmmaking has evolved over time.
- If a movie bombs, don't give up.
- Find a way to motivate your kids. We have some media boundaries in our home, so our kids did not expect to watch endless movies all summer. Thus, we framed the "extravaganza" as a compromise.
- Have fun. Don't worry if every discussion is not as deep as you'd like.

IF YOU'RE A YOUTH PASTOR OR MINISTER
Use movies to teach a biblical worldview

First, use movie clips in your teaching. Biblical themes are regularly found in movies, if you are willing to look for them.

Second, preach a series through film. There are many online articles and books that offer theological and worldview analyses of various films. You could analyze some recent movies or you could arrange the series around certain theological or apologetics questions. Find a creative approach and stick with it. To save time, you can show film clips instead of an entire movie.

Third, lead a regular movie group at your home. Serve food, watch different movies, and then discuss each film afterward. Read some articles ahead of time so you're prepared to ask good questions. This is a relational way to help students investigate truth.

IF YOU'RE A CHRISTIAN EDUCATOR
Incorporate modern media

If you teach Bible at a Christian school, try teaching a worldview unit that includes basic principles of critically approaching film and then watching various movies with students and discussing them. Keep a few things in mind:

- Use short movie clips if you do not have time to show an entire film.
- Show a variety of movies—comedy, action, science fiction, etc.—so students see that every film has a worldview.
- View Christian and non-Christian movies.
- Have students present their own worldview analysis of a film to the class.

If you teach another subject at a Christian school, set aside a weekly time to show a movie clip, YouTube video, popular meme, influential tweet, or other form of modern media that relates to your subject. For instance, have "Worldview Wednesday," "Film Fridays," or something similar. Make a connection between the media, your subject, and Scripture. Students will remember it and look forward to it.

GATHER YOUR THOUGHTS

Be an influencer of young people who seizes opportunities to help them engage culture effectively. But there is an important balance we want to stress: be careful not to exasperate the young. In other words, be careful not to overdo spiritual instruction. Finding a balance can be tricky, but the deeper you build relationships with youth, the more likely they will be to heed your instruction and not be provoked to annoyance. Young people need both truth and relationships.

> Fathers, do not provoke your children to anger, but bring them up in the discipline and instruction of the Lord. (Ephesians 6:4)

INCREASE YOUR UNDERSTANDING

Current events provide us with an important opportunity to teach Christian worldview. In *So the Next Generation Will Know*, chapter 8, "Love *Engages*," we describe three ways to examine, evaluate, and critique current events to engage students. Take notes specifically from the Current Events section found on pages 174–75.

We share stories of Christians _____:

We look for the Christian worldview _____:

We talk about _____:

NOTES

1. Christian Smith, *Soul Searching: The Religious and Spiritual Lives of American Teenagers* (New York: Oxford University Press, 2005), 89.

2. I (Sean) have personally heard reasons like these before. For similar responses and information, see *Gen Z: The Culture, Beliefs, and Motivations Shaping the Next Generation* (Ventura, CA: Barna Group, 2018).

3. To learn more about Brett Kunkle and his powerful ministry to young people (and to schedule your own worldview mission trip), please visit www.maventruth.com.